MY C

ISBN: 978-1-913642-22-8

Book designed by Aaron Kent

Edited by Aaron Kent

Broken Sleep Books (2021), Talgarreg, Wales

Contents

My Glorious Sundays

Aaron Kent

- Aaron Kent -

Foreword
by Tom Snarsky

What's your old-media memory? I will always love CDs for how they encouraged a kind of happening-into a band's body of work, like when the Need for Speed: Hot Pursuit 2 soundtrack led me to The Buzzhorn's album Disconnected (nearly forgotten now, but always a treasure). Another in this vein: getting the DGC Nirvana best-of one Christmas—simple black cover, shiny silver font—and reading all the liner notes before ever having heard, beyond the radio, a single Nirvana song. (We're beginning as My Glorious Sundays begins: with the album as, first, a gift.) It's an odd feeling to enter a band's oeuvre through the hybridity of the music itself plus words about the music—suddenly you're listening on a kind of alert, evaluatively, seeing if what you hear rings true to the writer's described experience of listening.

Aaron Kent subverts this aural/oral tension in My Glorious Sundays by playing both sides of the field. In your hands is not an objective, nonpartisan critical account of The Glorious Sundays' musical output; that might be interesting in its own right, but it isn't what Aaron's after. Instead you are holding a Künstlerroman written in parallel: the growth and development of a band alongside the growth and development of a person, their history and their sensibility. This growth dynamic is not unscary, as Aaron will tell you:

I guess that's the thing, though, innit? Like, how do you know what growth will do to you? It could be the beacon you hoped, this glorious [sic] thing that awakens a mood inside you that cannot and will not die.

The Glorious Sundays were driven by just such a mood, the "cannot and will not die" written into the overlapping journeys of the band members: Tommy Six and James Chase (and, a bit later on, Ammé Ron) continued to work together through lineup change after lineup change, through endless adjustments to and experimentation with their sound. As

- Aaron Kent -

a latecomer to TGS myself, my touchstone was Cedric and Omar of At the Drive-In/The Mars Volta/Antemasque/&c.: a musical partnership strong enough to grow together, warts (plus the odd schism-inducing feud) and all.

Just as Cedric and Omar co-wrought highs like Relationship of Command and Frances the Mute along with lows—is it fair to call them lows?—like Antemasque's "50,000 Kilowatts" (a deliciously absurd song I happily admit to loving dearly and finding immaculate, in its way), Tommy and James and Ammé worked together over years to build a genuine musical edifice: brilliant, unabashedly flawed, and sufficiently rich to support lifetimes of listening. As you read this book I hope Aaron's example of weaving himself into and through TGS's discography, a varied musical corpus strewn across 8 compact discs, brings to mind all the songs you wouldn't be yourself without. "I'd like to hear your spirit call", we hear James sing, midway through "A Motorway Thing" off the s/t. And as you turn this page, like cracking a new, sealed jewel case, you will.

Traversing the Equinox

2007

I guess a band like The Glorious Sundays doesn't come outta nowhere. We all gotta start somewhere, y'know. Like, James Chase didn't just call up Tommy Six one day and say *here we go, Tommy, we gone got ourselves one of those major record deals* without even having written a song.

Traversing the Equinox is to The Glorious Sundays what *Thank me Later* is to Drake, what *Subsequent Death* is to Aaron Kent, what 'Get Stoked on it!' is to The Wonder Years.[1] They don't wanna play those songs no more, they don't wanna talk about that album no more, and they don't wanna see that cover no more. But it's tough, a ton of people have the record, and you can't stop people listening to what they wanna listen to.

I was 18 when I picked it up, and honestly it was a bit of an error. My mate Flan Egan had asked for it as a birthday gift, had shown me the cover, and I got it. Only problem was they had shown me the cover for Modest Mouse's *We Were Dead Before the Ship even Sank* and I got it confused. Same blue, you see. So a couple days later I got him the right album, and kept this one.

> Traversing the Equinox
> better take two steps 'fore you take a shot
> traversing the equinox
> somewhere out there someone's left to rot
>
> — From the titular track on The Glorious Sundays' *Traversing the Equinox*

---

1   Stuck my own name in here, bit odd.

James Chase wrote all the words on the first album, and you can see that from the chorus, can't you? Like, he knew how to write a great verse, no doubt about it, but a chorus just weren't his thing. Who has been left to rot? Why take two steps before shooting? Is it the Wild West? Why is nobody burying the body? What's any of that got to do with the equinox? This is a shame, as the rest of the song - a battle-hardy hymn to staying out later until the streetlights came on - is almost garage-band perfection.

I was dating this girl, Marley, my first proper girlfriend, when I delved into this album.[2] We'd been together a year, and though I'd had girlfriends, this was my most serious one, not just some schoolyard anxiety-ridden thing. I'd burnt the album on my laptop and whatnot, stuck it on my Sony media player, and listened to it on the 30-minute train journey to her house, and the 30-minutes back.

I gotta think that she kinda tricked me. I was talking to a couple of different people at the time, and it was between Marley and Lucie that I was having trouble deciding. Not that I had a choice, 'cause it turned out Lucie weren't into me. But I also preferred Marley for several reasons: namely that Marley wasn't addicted to paracetamol, she played guitar, and she loved The Glorious Sundays. Only I later found out she'd had one guitar lesson two years prior, and had never heard of The Glorious Sundays, but had bought a ton of their stuff *after* we chatted to impress me. Kinda sweet, I guess.

---

2   Fake name, real person.

Marley smoked a lot of weed, which I didn't know until after we went official. She also phoned in the early hours after having cut herself. I'd stay on the phone until sunrise talking her through clean-up, soothing her to sleep, tiring myself. She tried to kick the weed, left her purse at my place intentionall. But then she'd do sexual favours for her dealer instead. I knew she was doing this, she admitted it, but I was weak and I didn't know what a relationship should've looked like. I don't think she did, either.

> Let's find ourselves new punchbags
> and change our point of view
> I'd blame it on myself if I
> wasn't so certain it was you
>
> — 'Sea-town' by The Glorious Sundays

I'm not completely innocent there, though; I cheated on her with Xamuel, my sorta-boss at the coffee shop at the time. I'd run away from home, got my own place and got a job making mocha for businessmen. Xamuel worked in the Plymouth branch, he was a manager, but he'd come down to cover for us in Truro occasionally. One night we all went out for drinks, and Xamuel and I played a game of chicken, an excuse for us to make out behind the Matalan car park. I was 16, he was 31.[3] I just really wanted a dad, I still do. I see father figures in everyone. First I want them to love me, then I want them to be proud of me, then I want them gone.

---

3   As I've got older I've come to see this encoutner for what it was: grooming.

Traversing the Equinox is a fine, if amateurish, debut. You can tell it's just James Chase and Tommy Six, sat in James' bedroom, noodling along with Tommy's acoustic guitar, and James' vocals. Some songs, such as 'Je Suis en Mer', are under-developed, poorly recorded, and bare not even the slightest hint of what was to come.[4]

I guess that's the thing, though, innit? Like, how do you know what growth will do to you? It could be the beacon you hoped, this glorious [sic] thing that awakens a mood inside you that cannot and will not die. Or it could be this harsh, dangerous, energy-sapping thing that eats you up.

---

4   The re-recorded version of this song is so different in so many ways that it's difficult to even conceive of this original version. Yet those first two lines 'So love me, mother, love me / Or don't love me, it's no crime / You can take me or leave / And you'll ignore me' are so similar to Frightened Rabbit's 'Music Now, that it's almost absurd to allow James Chase the chance to lie and say he hadn't heard the song before. Actually, even the title is stolen from Jacques Brel.

Marley and I eventually broke up. It wasn't easy. I blame her parents, and I blame(d) myself. She never knew how to love, or how to work as part of a unit, rather than as a single, self-preservatory thing. Her parents were attached in ways that meant even their own kids, Taylor and Marley, couldn't get in.[5] Her mother resented any time her father spent with either child, and demanded that she get his full attention. This led to her brother's control issues, as he spent hours determining what he could attach himself to in the absence of parents. His bedroom, a perfect stasis of him; his girlfriend, chained tightly to him; his sister, a piece of trash to discard.

> Call me home at the dawn of the internet
> steal me songs when I sing of my second-best
> I'm half-cut when you dress in your favourite dress
> I'm half-cut when you see me at my best
>
> 'Acts of Kindness by The Glorious Sundays'

---

5   They used to play Mario Kart, Marley's mum vs Marley's dad. The winner would get oral sex straight after. The kids would cheer their parents on - I always found that disconcerting, two kids cheering for which parent they want to be the recipient of oral sex.

Marley was angry, consistently hoping for a fight. She was violent: hitting me, smacking me, forcing me to the ground. She demanded things that were impossible to achieve. I still can't entirely work out the motive, what she got from us; if she wanted love, she didn't show that. The only time I came close to tenderness was whenever I threatened to leave. Those moments, deep in the fabrics of our relationship, so subtly weaved they were almost non-existent, they came like the apex of a storm. Marley, ten foot deep into prayer, swollen on her own regret, begging me to stay. And me, weakened like a door against a battering ram, hoping she'd finally change, knowing she wouldn't.

The final straw came when she *pikkatrapp pikkatrapp pikkatrapp* this gross, pulsating thing that hadn't been washed.[6] I left at night while she slept – my insomnia a friend for the first time. I sang loud on the drive home, traversing a new equinox.[7]

Don't eat my heart and tell me it's dinner

— 'It's Not the Same Person' by The Glorious Sundays

---

[6]   I originally wrote something here in place of the *pikatrapps,* and the first draft (seen by a few people) had the actual incident in it. But I've since deleted it. I guess shame is still the gremlin on my back.

[7]   Actually, this isn't true. I broke up with her to her face in the morning. She cried, claimed I was cheating on her with a Scottish girl at my university. I wasn't. I rang her mum who came and collected her while I packed away a few things. I came back a week or so later for the rest of my stuff. She rang me a few times over the next month, crying, but I was gone.

Self-titled

2009

1. SEA-TOWN
2. FULBRIGHT SCHOLARS
3. DIVINE MERCIES
4. THATCHER BURNS IN HELL
5. JE SUIS EN MER
6. WHERE THE BEE SUCKS
7. SONG FOR SECOND CHANCES
8. THE HOURS
9. A MOTORWAY THING
10. NO I IN TEAM
11. TONY THE PONY (BONUS TRACK)
12. SAY YES (ELLIOTT SMITH COVER)

The Glorious Sundays' eponymous sophomore release is a bit of a misnomer in their lengthy career – particularly given that they weren't a complete set just yet – so their self-titled album comes at the expense of not actually having the full band it is named after. Obviously, hindsight is 20/20, and they weren't to know they wouldn't stay a two-piece forever, but the title just seems a bit lazy and ill-thought out.[1] This is, however, James Chase and Tommy Six beginning to realise the sound they would grow to pioneer, the genre they would help to create, the music they would forever be remembered for. This is their first stab at plaincore.[2]

James Chase continued to provide vocals, but also laid down the bass tracks for the album, having been inspired to pick up the instrument by Mötley Crüe bassist Nikki Sixx at a young age. Tommy Six provides rhythm guitar, lead guitar, drums, and backing vocals. And for the first time, the songs are a process of work between James and Tommy, meaning James no longer determines the lyrics or music or the direction.

> Thatcher burns in hell
> Thatcher burns in hell
> Thatcher burns in hell
> Burn, Thatcher, burn
>
> —Thatcher Burns in Hell by The Glorious Sundays)

---

1   Rumoured potential titles turned down include: *The Glorious Basterds, Divinity in Small Mercies, Birthday Songs,* and (the frankly dreadful) *A Tale for Tenderness*.
2   James Chase is on record stating that he hates this genre title; 'I just think it ignores the beauty of the band working under this guise. To determine them as plain means people assume it isn't innovative, whereas I'd argue it's more innovative than most genres.'

When I was a little kid, I dunno, like eight or so, my dad started to project his Tory sensibilities upon me. It became something of a game for him, I think, to politicise his children. He has, probably, a 25% success rate now, only one of my brothers admitting to giving the Tory scum a cross on the paper. The others have voted Tory during their lives, but as they got older and wiser they began to think for themselves. I can imagine my dad doesn't like this. I wouldn't know.[3]

So, as a young'un I was taught that Tony Blair was the enemy – which, sure, the man was a Tory posing as a Labour Prime Minister, so my dad was right, just not in the way he thought he was. I was taught that the Tories had the best interests of the country at large in mind, and I was taught that Margaret Thatcher was the best thing to have happened to this country.

> She's the greatest leader this country ever had
> tell your teacher that
>
> — My dad, some mornings before I'd leave for school

I'd do it. I'd tell my friends how great Thatcher was, I told my teachers about her brilliance, and I'd convince myself, too. But the thing is, I didn't know anything about her, or her politics. I just parroted what I'd been taught to parrot, and when my English teacher fought back, I learnt to despise my English teacher, which meant I became unfocused and disinterested in a subject I've since grown to love and teach.[4]

---

3   I don't have any contact with my parents or brothers anymore.
4   I actually didn't learn about semantic fields because of this: at 12 or so my dad had taught me to hate the anybody left of right wing and my teacher was left wing. She did a bit on semantic fields and I just didn't work at all. So it wasn't until I redid my A Levels that it clicked.

Imagine being from a mining community and telling everyone you know that the person who burned down your future is your Messiah.

I don't know a lot about Skullbone Records, but I bought this album the moment it was released.[5] Here was this underground band I adored, finally snapped up by an indie label, releasing their first set of recordings from a studio. The sound was suddenly punchy, imbued with sonic slap that their music hadn't had before. They'd gone fully electric and I was excited.

The new versions of 'Sea-Town', and 'Je Suis en Mer' were fascinating, remarkable for their sound enhanced by the studio, and their lyrics shifted – potentially to avoid a lawsuit in one case. 'A Song for Second Chances' had the pop-rock vibe of The Front Bottoms, and 'A Motorway Thing' had all the absurdity of early Titus Andronicus boiled down to a three minute chunk.

> I'm shoulder deep in your swimming pool
> holding on so I don't drown
> I'd like to hear your spirit call
> I'd like to see you come down
>
> — A Motorway Thing by The Glorious Sundays

Though most of the album is essentially flawless, there is one track that I'd argue would be better forgotten. 'Fulbright Scholars' is a frankly meandering track, bored by its own futility, ignorant of its own failing premise. Tommy Six, rumour has it, hated it from the start, yet James Chase was certain that it was a song that had to be heard.

---

5   Due to a lack of searchable information about the label, it's difficult to tell whether it was written as 'Skullbone Records' or 'SkullboneRecords' as both feature at the bottom of the back cover.

My dad knew what he was doing, and he did it with glee. The S*n newspaper scattered around the house, the Daily Mail occasionally on the sofa, Tory leaflets on the doorstep.[6] He sucked it all up with wild abandon. If anything, the Tories weren't right enough for him, he wanted more, and so did my mum. Immigrants were an issue. Benefit claimants were an issue. Single mothers were an issue. Issues become problems. Problems need solutions. Societal solutions are rarely non-violent.

Our neighbours, three doors up, joined the then-unknown UKIP political party. I had no idea who they were, but I knew my dad admired them. They had stickers on the window declaring the UK to be British, and Britain in need of English standards. It was a confused stance, one further compounded by their inability to grasp sovereignty and its reach. They felt the Queen was some sort of symbol for the nation that could ensure prosperity for white people. They couldn't begin to understand the irrelevance of her powers.

I can't remember when I stepped away from the cultish territory of my parent's politics – the clasping claw of their fevered anger no longer tearing at me.

---

6   As a kid I used to cover page 3 when I read The Scum, I used to put my hand over the topless woman and read the articles around it. I was convinced that I was gay because of the jokes and jibes made about this impulse of mine. Turns out I'm pan, but I don't think covering The S*n's shitty propoganda nudity is a sign of sexual preference.

I spoke to an old school friend years later, a friend who couldn't believe I wasn't a Tory. He was shocked at the way my father had controlled me, and he questioned how much it could be defined as brainwashing.[7]

7   To be fair, he was Labour because his dad was, so not much better but at least he's not a Tory.

James Chase went through a Ted Hughes phase, obsessed with *Birthday Letters*, a book that is disconcerting in its seeming equivalence of profit with suicide. Ted had, it was, driven Sylvia Plath to her suicide – and if he hadn't driven her to it, then he certainly hadn't given her a safe home or partner in their marriage. *Birthday Letters*, written as memories of Sylvia, are problematic in the sense that they allowed Ted to increase his value as a creative idol through the glorification of a relationship that was deeply flawed. Tommy Six had concerns about this, but James Chase was adamant in his desire to release 'Fulbright Scholars', a track named after the very first poem in the collection.

> Peaches
> fresh for the first time
> you, me
> dressed to our worst nines'
>
> — Fulbright Scholars by The Glorious Sundays

This may have been the closest The Glorious Sundays came to breaking up in those early days, the arguments reaching such a pitch that James and Tommy refused to speak to each other for several days. Here they were, under the management of a record label, their dreams of recording an album in a studio realised, and Ted bloody Hughes is causing them grief.

James has, in various interviews, recalled one moment where he told Tommy to fuck off, that he didn't need him, that he could find somebody else. Tommy, apparently, returned the insult with similarly firm words, telling James that he could die, or go see a shrink, some sorta thing where you can fuck off and think. Those lines, now immortalised in the final seconds of 'Fulbright Scholars': a stab at Ted Hughes, but also a barb at themselves.

Tommy eventually gave up defending Ted Hughes, realising that he should perhaps build his own mystique rather than rely on somebody else's.

This Gold Season

2010

This Gold Season (sometimes stylised as THIS.GOLD.
SEASON) was the first EP by The Glorious Sundays. Riding
high off the acclaim, and growing fanbase, of their self-titled
release, the band recorded the EP to ensure they wouldn't slip
out of focus. This, also, was an opportunity to record as a full
band, no longer just James Chase and Tommy Six, but with
the introduction of Ammé Ron on bass, and the mononymous
Rant on drums.

There are a few interesting points to make about the cover
of the album, in that it was clearly their most professional
looking work to date, designed by James Chase. James had
designed the previous covers, the clip-art looking Traversing
the Equinox, and the punk minimalism of the self-titled
release. Yet, *This Gold Season* looked shiny and professional:
like a band who had given up on amateur hijinks. Also to note
is the spelling of 'Terra Firma' as 'Terrafirma' a decision that
led some fans to believe it was a simple error, but others to
define it as the band finally coming together as a whole: the
terrain meeting solid ground, the connection between all
parts creating a firmness that hadn't previously existed.

Ammé had known James and Tommy for some time,
having been a fan of the band in the early days. She went
to college with both of them and, for a short period, ran
their merch stand at local gigs. She was a far better bass
player than James, and while he was hesitant to give up the
instrument, the freedom imposed by not being shackled
to the stage meant he could perfect the stage persona that
eventually went on to become a defining feature of himself
and the band.

Rant, however, was a different breed altogether. Nowhere
near as talented, or focused, as Ammé, not as determined as
James, not even as sensitive and receptive as Tommy. Rant
was a misnomer in the group, pure animalistic energy, pure
alcoholic evenings.

Stella!
Stella can you hear me
I've been calling clearly
Stella can you hear me

— Streetcar by The Glorious Sundays

I assumed something was deeply wrong with me from a very young age.[1] There were these things about myself I couldn't control, little moments, or grand characteristics. I hadn't noticed them in other kids, and it became more and more clear that they were part of the building blocks that made me whole. If I removed one then I would come crashing down.

It wasn't until I was in my early 20s that I was diagnosed with ADHD which finally meant I had a reason for my incessant, and frankly annoying, energy. Those times when my whole body felt like an orb of and I needed to jolt, or yelp, or jump, now made sense. It didn't change anything, I would still infuse a room with energy to the point of annoyance. I'd still have times where I'd be telling myself *you're such a fucking idiot, calm down, dumbass*. I still hated myself.

When Rant joined The Glorious Sundays, I finally had somebody I could look up to, somebody who had ADHD like me but had made it.[2]

> I'm breaking ground in broken sleep
> you hold me close, I start to weep /
> this is the year I stand my ground
> this is the year I'm swinging proud
> Winter made me rearrange
> and I'm calling my own shots
> I'm counting all my bullets
> and I'm coming out tops'
>
> — Terrafirma by The Glorious Sundays

Look, I can't say the drumming particularly stood out to me when I bought the EP. It wasn't like Rant became my sole focus, or that it was serendipitous in my discovery of the band and then him. But I watched a short interview of the

---

1   To be honest, I still think there's something wrong with me.
2   TGS never said Rant had ADHD, but Rant hinted at it several times.

band, and Rant just couldn't sit still: he was fidgety, like me, and he was annoying, like me.

This Gold Season is a strong EP, and while the tracks didn't fit with the next album, they held their own in the three-track format. *T.G.S* was a transient EP, a short step between the self-titled record and *Melodies for Enemies!*. The shortest track on the record, 'Grace', is six and a half minutes long. The longest, *'Terrafirma'*, is just shy of ten minutes. But it doesn't ever feel like a luxurious, or wanky album, the tracks are, instead, necessary examinations of the here and then. There are no overlong solos or misguided silences, each track is all killer, no filler.[3]

James Chase finds new levels of rage and despair. His blood boils over in the middle of 'Stella' as he screams for the father that abandoned him, and his voice whimpers at the end of 'Terrafirma' as he begs the therapy to work. Tommy Six channels Bloc Party; chords drawn out, notes ringing in pure emotion, the moments he chooses not to play just as integral as the moments when he does. Ammé Ron brings a melody that the band had been missing, the piece they never knew they needed. She helps the band find their groove, and shows why The Glorious Sundays are known as a three-piece not just Tommy and James.

---

3   To use a phrase from Sum 41's ironically titled album.

Rant, though. Rant was kinda unhinged.[4]

---

4   That's harsh. Calling him unhinged is unfair. He was an alcoholic, but at that moment in time he hadn't fully given into his demons, he was in that partying stage: *I'll just have one to liven the night up.*

I actually feel sorry for him now, well, at least with regards to the alcoholism, not for what he did to Tommy Six. I've always been wary of alcohol, my Grandad is an alcoholic. I started drinking a beer every so often to calm down from stressful days, just a can to take the edge off at the end of the night. Just on Fridays and Saturdays.

Then it was also Sundays, cause, y'know, the weekend.

Then it was five nights a week.

Then it wasevery night.

I drank a beer every night for six months, and though that's not exactly heavy, it's still 30 beers or so a month.

I'm down in quantity now; I drink like two a week maybe. But I have moments where I see beer, whether in a petrol station, or via the incessant emails I get from Flavourly or Beer52, and I feel like I need one. And I usually cave.

I've stopped and started over the last few months.

I'd really like to stop.[5]

5   (I WROTE THIS FOOTNOTE PRIOR TO MY BRAIN BLEED, IT READS DIFFERENTLY TO ME NOW)

Tommy Six had been engaged for almost a year when Rant joined the band. The story goes that James dated Sally in year 11. They lasted a week. James barely remembers the relationship, but he sats he cried when she broke up with him on the seventh day. Tommy recalls it slightly differently, believing that he spoke to James about it first, telling him *I dunno, man, it just feels right between Sally and me*. They weren't that close at the time, and it caused further shifts that delayed the formation of The Glorious Sundays.

When Tommy decided to start a band, he kept coming back to the idea of James, having heard him sing in school. They were in college together but rarely spoke, and Tommy was worried that James would flat out turn him down. Karma for Sally.[5]

After one rehearsal, the band was set. James never spoke to Sally, but they didn't like each other much anyway.

---

6   The demo of 'Karma for Sally' was released three years after *This Gold Season*, on the fan-site thegloriousnet.com. Tommy was still, clearly, angry about her betrayal, and the lack of drums on the track speaks volumes. It's just Tommy on acoustic guitar, Ammé on a five string acoustic bass, and James singing as tenderly as he could.

I saw The Glorious Sundays live for the first time shortly after the release of *This Gold Season*. They hadn't made the trip down to Cornwall to support their previous two albums, having spent time on their local pub circuit for *Traversing the Equinox*, and hitting University bars in the bigger cities for their self-titled album. Yet, ICHLFAF Records had enough of a budget to send them further afield for *This Gold Season,* and I snapped up tickets as soon as they went on sale.

My friend Marc and I turned up early. We wanted to catch the support act Underdream as they had something of a following in the local scene. They were underwhelming, getting stuck in a rut on most songs that sounded absolutely mundane. We weren't sure what the fuss was about, and we left to go to the bar before the end of their set, to top up our drinks.

At the bar we heard rumours that Rant was buying rounds of drinks entirely for himself, slamming back shots, and generally doing all he could to get pissed. I'd heard he was a bit of an alcoholic, but I assumed it was all part of his persona.

> Call it Grace, call it composure
> call it calm, call it closure
>
> —'Grace' by The Glorious Sundays

I was proven wrong the moment he got on stage. The guitar rang out for 'Terrafirma', Tommy Six on stage, holding a note, bringing the rest of the band out. James Chase grabbed the mic and stood as close to the crowd as he could, Ammé already looking for her cleanest route into the hundred or so people. But, Rant leaned against a pillar in the back, his ass barely on his drumstool, his head slumped forward. He was unconscious, and he was sliding to the floor.

Even writing this I can't stop tapping my leg, or fiddling with things. It's like my body has this innate need to be doing *something, anything*.

I assumed the ADHD was also the reason for my moods, why I spent time yo-yoing between sheer energy, excitement, and positivity, to despair, depression, and suicidal thoughts. I thought my body was releasing too much energy at unnecessary times, so when I ran out of the store I had the crash came with a downturn in mood.

Eventually, I decided to go back to the doctors, where he sent me onto CAHMS who took tests, spoke to me, delved into my very being, and determined I had Borderline Personality Disorder. They set up a meeting for me to talk it through, but I never went back, too scared of a diagnosis to understand how to achieve it.

It was around that time I realised it wasn't Rant I felt connected to, it was James.

> 'I'm dreaming of car crashes again / I dreaming of disaster, I'm dreaming of the end / and I'm praying for it to come true'
>
> (Streetcar by The Glorious Sundays)

Rant was just a party-maniac, he just wanted to drunk, fight, fuck, sleep, repeat. It wasn't that he had made it despite his issues, it was just that he had an aura people found alluring. Yet, he'd eventually drain those around him, weakening their resolve before leaving forever.[6]

---

6   See footnote 4.

Melodies for Enemies!

2011

MELODIES FOR ENEMIES!

Or, how the gentle ache of existence grew into a cacophony of anguish so loud that the only way to stop it was to end things

1. **Melodies for Enemies** (3:15) [Chase, Six, Ron]

2. **Stupid Reasons** (3:25) [Six, Chase]

3. **Promeande** (1:00) [Chase, Six, Ron]

4. **Sertraline &** (6:36) [Chase]

5. **Reasons to Trust a Fortnight** (4:11) [Chase, Ron, Six]

6. **No Saviours** (5:50) [Six, Chase, Ron]

7. **O! Bleeding Drops of Red** (2:59) [Chase]

8. **Cacophony** (9:02) [Chase]

9. **Intrusive Obsession** (3:54) [Chase, Six, Ron]

10. **The Old Man, The Boats** (4:36) [Chase, Six, Ron]

11. **Fin** (0:52) [Ron]

ICHLFAF records, 17 St Solturf Road, 5th floor, Manchester. M1
Cover design by: James Chase
Catalog no. 02061989
Copyright (2011) ICHLFAF RECORDS

I mean, if you don't include *Traversing the Equinox* as an official release, which is understandable considering it was distributed to very few record stores, and was just two guys mucking about at home, then *Melodies for Enemies!* is The Glorious Sundays' sophomore effort.[1] With *TtE* having been released – self-released even – in 2007, and this record in 2011, the band were averaging an album once every couple years, which is industry standard.

There were rumours that one or all of the songs from *This Gold Season* would make it onto *MfE!!,* but after Rant's unceremonious departure, it was easier to produce completely new material and leave the ghost behind them. That and the influence of Rant ran heavy through the album – just not musically.

New drummers came and went: John Murphy, Yoshi Kenjo, and Jamie Jamie all play on tracks on the album, which gives the LP a discordant appeal, a band in flux. But I've always felt like that was the charm of *MfE!!*, this kind of strange disconnection between tracks.

> Keep it together, it's only getting better
> but these words they don't seem to make sense
> so I try to play it cool when all that I can do
> is think of all the stupid reasons that I never really was into you'
>
> — 'Stupid Reasons' by The Glorious Sundays

---

1   I don't know how a copy of *Traversing the Equinox* ended up in a record store in Truro, Cornwall, but I guess the guy who ran it was a big fan of showing off his knowledge of underground bands. I know a bunch of small groups from across the country used to send demos down in the hope they'd get stocked; maybe this is how it worked with TGS too.

I joined the Navy at 20, so around the time TGS released their self-titled album, and I was in for a couple years before I was medically discharged. *MfE!!* came out around the time I was back to being a civvy.

I'd never wanted to join the military, I still hate the fact that I did, but I was desperate. I was still with Marley and wanted a way out. My job had given me a promotion, but the recession took that position away, and my old job had been filled. I was broke, I was scared, and I was easily led. So I went into the recruitment office, under Marley's advice, and decided to become a SONAR operator on nuclear submarines.

I don't really want to go much into my time in the services.[2] I passed my marksman's test, even though I'm anti-gun and had never used one before. I went to America on the submarine, which was cool, I guess. And I was violently sexually assaulted by a warrant officer while onboard.

---

2   I actually really dislike the military, am anti-Trident, and hate warfare altogether.

Prior to *MfE!!* - or during the initial recordings depending on who you believe - Rant became homeless. He hadn't paid his rent for a few months, and was essentially looking at slumming it on the benches at his local train station. So Tommy Six, being the kind-hearted guy he is, took him in. Sally hated Rant, so there were plenty of arguments between Tommy and Sally, but Tommy won out and Rant came to stay.

I don't know how obvious this is, but Rant started an affair with Sally. I mean, it was destined to happen, come on, they hate each other, they live together... you've seen movies before.

James Chase had mostly removed himself from the day-to-day personal lives of the band. He was struggling with his borderline personality disorder diagnosis, and the songs on *MfE!!* are probably the most clear indication of his intentions. Ammé has spoken fairly openly about her concerns for him at the time in an interview with *Post-Post-Music Mag*:

> I walked in to his home, having not heard from him in a while, and he wasn't home. I looked around, because the door was open, but he had obviously just upped and left. Then, I smelt something odd, and followed it to the garage where he was trying to off himself with carbon monoxide.

— Ammé Ron, *Post-Post-Music Mag*)

Ammé focused her attentions on James, helping him to find some stability, meaning Tommy was alone to deal with the mess enveloping his home and his life. He discovered the affair, and still let Rant live with him, too kind and too meek to kick him out. He decided to divorce Sally, and Rant moved into Tommy's bed. [3]

---

3   Rant left one night without a word to anybody, which both Sally and Tommy were fine with. Sally had stopped their affair after a week or two after Tommy's discovery and subsequent divorce demands, and Tommy had fired Rant from the band, a decision James and Ammé weren't aware of but would later support when they found out. Sally went on to date some local guy, all the while still living with Tommy while they arranged the sale of Tommy's half to Sally and her new man.

1.	In the Navy there are several training aspects before you can effectively qualify for your trade.
2.	The first is initial training at HMS Raleigh, which in and of itself is traumatic.[4] nine weeks of early wake-ups, constant beastings, pure competition, and violence as a training exercise.
3.	Then, as a SONAR rating, you do 20-plus weeks of training in HMS Raleigh at the Submarine School. This part isn't so bad, it's a bit more chilled, and you're given more freedom. But you don't move straight over to start, there's a little gap of a few weeks, plus we had summer in the middle of initial training.
4.	So at the end of all this training at HMS Raleigh, you've been in the Navy for almost a year and you've still not stepped foot on a submarine. You're trained entirely as a submarine surrogate.
5.	Then you move up to HMS Faslane.[5]

4	A couple of things really spring to mind here. There was an incident where one of the traiNEES ran into the shower brandishing a hot iron and pressed it against another trainee's bare ass. The flesh melted and slapped to the floor, bits of blood and flesh pooling in the drain.

Before we joined there was a trainee who was struggling with the intensity of initial training, so he went to the toilets in the early hours of the morning and slit his wrists. Then he slit his throat. When this didn't kill him he instantly jumped out of the window. I slept in the bed he had previously occupied.

5	This doesn't happen straightaway either, I ended up working in a forces career office for a month or so before I moved up.

When The Glorious Sundays finally got round to finding the mental space to record, they started with their most famous song, 'Stupid Reasons'. James Chase wrote most of the songs on the album, and they primarily occupied the dark/beautiful crossover Chase is famous for, but *Stupid Reasons* was conceived by Tommy Six. He'd written the music after finally getting a place away from Sally, and although he hummed the rough melody, the chorus was completely written by him. Chase would later add the verse lyrics, but it was a Six song.[6]

Six also wrote the majority of 'No Saviours' but it is widely believed that Six's original version bears little resemblance to the final version, and widely believed that the final, Chase-edited, version is much better, even if he did drag it out an extra two minutes.

Chase's research and increased reading begins to show up here, a hobby he picked up while isolating himself from the world. There's a hint of Walt Whitman in *'O! Bleeding Drops of Red'*, so named after the line from 'O Captain My Captain', and there's a reference to Emily St John Mandel's 'Station Eleven' in 'Cacophony'. Perhaps, though, Chase's lyrical ability is at its most literary when he isn't even referencing literature; 'The Old Man, The Boats' is an extraordinary feat with Chase's haunting lyrics backed by Tommy Six's gentle piano and Ammé Ron's brushed drums.

> 'I'd rather be the fish than the fisherman
> The loaded sky, two barrels into a fever'd plan
> spitting teeth at the bedroom window'
>
> — 'The Old Man, The Boats' by The Glorious Sundays

---

6   This was most likely why it is their biggest hit, with nearly 500 million streams on Spotify alone. Six had a better grasp of what was necessary for pop sensibilities, and he could write 'catchy' in his sleep – hence the classic *woah oh ohs* in the refrain.

Recording sessions were a veritable mix of influences, with each of the members (sans the rotating drummers) leaning towards different influences, different styles. Tommy Six began his love affair with The Beatles here, falling away from his previous love of heavier riffs (a la Rage Against the Machine). James Chase began to delve into late-stage post-emo music, absorbing the words of bands such as La Dispute, and Pianos Become the Teeth. Finally, Ammé Ron had The Wonder Years' new effort *Suburbia I've Given You All and Now I'm Nothing* on constant repeat.

I've gotta think that the mix of influences here made the album what it is, a musical masterpiece.

6. At Faslane, a naval base on the outskirts of the west of Scotland, you have to undertake more training: SMQ Dry. SMQ Dry is the submariner's qualification undertaken on dry land. The idea is to begin to understand the full operation of every aspect of the submarine.

7. After you pass your Dry training, you get assigned to some SONAR suite, where you train a bunch of officers who couldn't give two shits about you, while Channel 5 pops in to film them for some rat-ass TV show.

8. Finally, after nearly 18 months in the military, you get onboard a Submarine to undertake SMQ Wet: a logbook of qualifications for every aspect of the submarine, each of which has to be signed off by a higher rank who has better things to do than quiz you on a hydraulic valve number.

9. Before you can take your final test with a board of officers who spend hours testing your entire database of submarine knowledge, you have to do walkarounds. These take place in the fwd, mid, aft. You need some higher rank to agree to spend some hours away from his bunk to walk you around and confirm your knowledge. These higher ranks don't love it because there's nothing in it for them.

10. Unless... unless you get the guy who wants to take you down to AMS 2/3, stick his hands in your pants, smack you around, and tickle your dick.

The album ends with 'Fin', a 52 second instrumental from Ammé Ron that packs in more emotion than all the other tracks combined.[7] It is direct, cutting, full of brevity, and majestically light. The string section is intentionally underused to make way for the solo trumpet, and the piano's singular key somehow manages to convey the album's themes with a single note.

Without 'Fin' the album would never have felt finished.

---

7   Which isn't to say the other tracks have no emotion – they do. It's just they're a 10/10, and 'Fin' is a 12/10.

Exposition de Misère

2013

Exposition de Misère is the first The Glorious Sundays album with Onej Tuocs on drums, and it really feels complete. Onej would go on to join the band, but their work on *EdM* was initially intended to be as a session drummer, though the vibe caught them and they became a permanent member of TGS, both on tour and in the studio.

That's not to say there wasn't tension in the band or drama, but they were working on a creative wavelength none of them had ever experienced before. James Chase would later call *EdM* 'the very first time I knew we were going to make it.'

The vinyl release of *EdM* came with a bonus cassette of conversations in the studio. These dialogues contained hints of the dynamics at play within the band, little creative successes and arguments. But listening back a few things are clear:

1. Tommy Six is considering leaving the band at the start of the sessions.
2. James Chase and Amme are hooking up.
3. Onej Tuocs has huge influence despite being considered a session musician.
4. James Chase is not looking after himself: too much coffee, too much alcohol, not enough sleep.
5. *EdM* is the reason Tommy stays in the band.

The first time I depersonalised was when I was 12 in Design Technology class. The memory is a blur, but I know, looking back, that I felt something was wrong. I didn't depersonalise after that for almost a year, until I was stood on a balcony in Spain, 13 years old, deciding that I would jump to my death.[1]

When *Exposition de Misère* came out I was depersonalising heavily and often. I was working night shifts at the Asda in St Austell, going through the motions. It felt like I was behind a screen, watching myself perform menial tasks, disconnected from my physical self.

The world ceased to exist in the solid, lucid form I had knew, and while I assumed it was a side effect of a lifetime of insomnia, it became apparent that it was, in fact, something deeper and more troubling.

---

1   There was a tent, like a massive food tent, below. We were on the seventh or eighth floor, and I was planning how to avoid the tent. At 12. Planning how to kill myself easiest.

I was four minutes into ' A Dictionary of Broken Wings' during a midnight drive when I decided to kill myself.

This is the path adventure brings
this is the reason the blackbird sings
this is a call for ominous things
this is a dictionary of broken wings'

— A Dictionary of Broken Wings by The Glorious Sundays

It's never quite been stated why Tommy Six was considering leaving TGS. Some surmised that his reluctance to continue began when the band refused to veer towards the pop sensibilities he was indulging in with his newfound love of The Beatles. This rift between styles would later be quashed in one of the extensive band meetings they had; James Chase was more intrigued by the styling of bands like Bloc Party; those swirling walls of harmonious noise, whereas Amme Ron had latched onto Young Fathers.

The clash of styles is what makes *Exposition de Misère* so good, it's a symbiotic relationship of genres hammered into a delicate balance. No part sounds too different to be discordant, but they never find themselves beating the same drum. It's in the differences that *EdM* comes alive, and where TGS produce what is clearly their magnum opus, their masterpiece.

There's a moment, about 15 seconds before the end of 'But Now the Fox,' where if you listen closely, you can hear a yelp of excitement from somebody in the studio, a sort of giddy shout of glee. Some critics felt it was intentional, the band chose to record the noise and lay it over the track. But others saw it as a spontaneous burst of in-studio joy. If the official TGS fansite is to be believed, then it's Tommy Six declaring his love for the song and the entire project.[2]

---

2   Tommy Six had a connection with Onej Tuocs that became clear during the recording of 'But Now the Fox'. That giddy yelp is Six's uncontrolled excitement at feeling conected to the band again, musically.

I saw a Matthew Perry film once where he played this guy who smokes weed one night and ends up with depersonalisation disorder.[3] The weed did it. It threw me off for a while because I've never tried drugs; between the night terrors and depersonalisation I always felt I didn't need an extra hit of surrealism. But Matthew Perry was just a normal guy who developed DPD because of drugs, and that's a real shitty way to look at a mental disorder.[4] I think my depersonalisation disorder came about from a lifetime of failing to acknowledge or deal with recurrent abuses. I stayed with Marley for 7 years even though she was awful and violent and mentally abusive. I bottled up the sexual assault I suffered in the military. I just refused to come to terms with any of these things, instead choosing to let them simmer in a mind that wasn't prepared to turn the heat off.

---

3   The film is Numb, directed by Harris Goldberg.
4   Turns Harris Goldberg has DPD, so maybe smoking weed at the wrong time might change some mental faculties and distort reality in a permanent state.

On that night drive, just two months shy of leaving Marley for good, I depersonalised bad. The world was unfathomable as a component of reality, everything had phantasmagoric edges, I was unstable and completely lost somewhere a couple of feet behind my bones. I was bored and tired of everything, but mostly of being unable to connect with life as a substance. I wanted to feel something, regardless of what that something was, and I wanted to come to terms with the reality vs construction debate that raged in my lucid moments. So I decided to drive my car into a wall: a large, thick, brick wall that separated the road from an immense drop. 'A Dictionary of Broken Wings' had reached its apex, that whirlwind of guitar that increased in tempo as James Chase sung 'there's a break inside the depth of me / and I don't want to leave here haunted' over and over and over, increasing with the tempo of the song, the runaway train it had become. I knew that by hitting the wall I would (hopefully) die and lose the incessant battle against reality that plagued me, and the idea warmed me. Sure, there was a chance that I would be left in great pain in hospital, but at least that would demonstrate the solidity of reality. I'd made up my mind: I was going to die, and The Glorious Sundays would soundtrack it.

James Chase had always found it difficult to stray from temptation - not in sordid ways like drugs or an affair but rather in terms of indulgence. Coffee was a habit he failed to kick, downing multiple double espressos during the recording of *Exposition de Misère*. He was rumoured to drink between five and 10 cups of black coffee in the six-hour recording sessions, and occasionally chase them with an energy drink. His alcohol intake increased after the sessions, and he was clearly failing to care for his health in the manner he should.

Amme, on the other hand, had always been keen to put her health, both mental and physical, before anything else. Yoga was compulsory for her before even stepping foot in the studio, and the only drinks she touched were water and herbal teas. So when James Chase and Amme Ron began seeing each other, it was a surprise to the entire band, and their adoring fans.

One particular conversation, on the bonus cassette, hinted at Amme's dislike of James' dietary habits, her loathing of his coffee-all-day, alcohol-all-night routine. He regularly played basketball so remained in shape, but the toll of the caffeine and alcohol was beginning to affect his behaviour in frustrating ways for the band.

Amme, having been the one to pull him from the car during his lowest point, had seemingly taken it upon herself to try to steer him towards good habits.

> Cassie Collins, you took me home
> you stole me from the end
> oh Cassie how could I not see
> how deep I could depend
> on you ba ba ba ba
> on you ba ba ba ba
> cassie I depend
> until the very end I will run with you'
>
> (Cassie Collins by The Glorious Sundays)

James Chase had wrote 'Cassie Collins' during the recording sessions when it became clear there wouldn't be enough songs on the record for an album. The songs mostly ran over six or seven minutes, so a 9th track would tip it into album territory.

Tommy Six let slip, in an interview with *Rock Sound,* that the lyrics were originally about Amme. 'When he first played that song, "oh Amme how could I not see". Shit, I mean Cassie.' The jig was up. Amme and James were in a relationship, and there was a real sense of relief from all four members of the band that they no longer needed to hide it.[5]

---

5   It's never been made clear why they felt the need to hide it. Their fanbase wouldn't have abandoned them, and the band were happy for them. The general belief is that it was merely a fleeting paranoia.

I steered away from the wall at the very last second, skidding back onto the road and spinning out on the tarmac. I gathered myself and drove to the next lay-by, where I parked, turned the engine off, and sobbed.

On the side of the road, I cried relentlessly. I thought about myself as a kid, the ugly little pain-in-the-ass I was. I thought about how weak I was, my inability to do anything for myself beyond staying in situations I hated. I hated myself for being annoying, for being that person who has too much energy and goes over the top. I was filled with absolute rage at Aaron Kent, the body and soul of whom I hated, passionately.

I stepped out of the car and looked at the empty dual carriageway. I couldn't kill myself properly; I was an utter failure. I was so ashamed of myself that I considered lying in the road, on the darkest point, and waiting to be run over. Instead, I punched myself in the face, hard.

I don't know if you've ever punched yourself, but it isn't as easy as it sounds. The main problem is that you know the punch is coming, so your instincts take over to avoid it at full throttle. That and its hard to punch yourself as hard as you probably deserve to be punched.

It took a few warm up punches to build up the momentum to crack myself in the right side of the face with a decent punch.

I went back to the car and put *EdM* on. I listened to 'Silence A Present A Promise' on repeat until I couldn't absorb it any more. In Walter Moers' *The 13½ Lives of Captain Bluebear* there is a gelatinous prince from a different dimension who eats music. I was that prince.

> At twilight with low light
> I don't need a fistfight
> I don't want the streetlights
> I just want the sweet night

> — 'Silence A Present A Promise' by The Glorious Sundays

The next day I watched the Richard Curtis film *About Time,* and I watched Domnhall Gleeson discover that time travel means his children will be different children. By altering the past his kids were not the kids he knew. I watched the desperation of his attempt to revert his error, and the joy upon succeeding and holding his kids again. I knew I wanted children and I wanted a love that wasn't sworn in by violence. I knew Marley was far removed from these aspirations, and I had to be courageous for the first time.

Just a couple weeks after breaking up with Marley I went to a Halloween party. I was dressed as a monkey and I won several games of beer pong. The host had The Glorious Sundays on his party mixtape, but only the classics. After the party ended, just beyond midnight, several people decided to go into Truro to grab some food and head to the clubs. On the way into the city centre a friend asked if I wanted to get a beefburger, and I told him I didn't as I was vegetarian. Behind me a tipsy zombie shouted: 'No way I'm vegetarian too and my mums are lesbians.' We chatted the whole way to Vanilla.[6] Her name was Emma and I was captivated by her.

We got married within three and a half years, and had two children by 2020.[7]

_____

6   Vanilla is a Cornish nightclub in Truro. I'd never been before meeting Emma. I didn't end up going in that night. My younger brother had been kicked out as I was queued up to go in, so I got him home and crashed into bed.

7   Odd to think that had I hit that wall none of this would have happened. I had made plans, packed stuff away, written a note, cleaned myself up, trimmed my beard, and left everything in a reasonable condition for whatever came after my death. Turns out what was to come was a compete reversal.

- Aaron Kent -

New Episode Every Sunday

2015

To start on a negative, this is by far my least favourite TGS cover and title. It's so cheap and lazy to have gone for a connection between the band name and TV episodes being released on Sunday; it almost feels as if they found a stock photo of a TV, stuck text over it and called it a day.

That said, this album holds a special place in my heart. It's by no means their best, hell I wouldn't even put it in my top five, but it was released during a particularly complex period of my life and has woven itself into the fibres of that space.

I was coming to terms with who I was, what I had been through and the traumas so steeped in darkness that suicide felt like the most sensible option. Emma was the first person I had spoken to about my abuse, the sexual assault, the sexual abuse, the history of violence, and she guided me in a way she never should have had to. She was, and still is, precious in ways I can't ever allow myself to be. The very soul of her being wrapped up in the many ways she could conceive of manifesting love and light for those around her. I (and I still feel guilty about this) burdened her with my truth, with my stories. She wanted to know who I was at my core, and it got to a point where I felt comfortable to finally share with somebody, and she felt secure enough to allow me to attach. But that said, the best decision she took was to encourage therapy first and foremost above everything.

My first therapist didn't work out, neither did the second or third. I felt like giving in but Emma found Cornwall Rape and Sexual Abuse Centre, CRASAC, and there I took the first steps on a path to forgiveness and clarity that seemed so removed previously. On my first drive to CRASAC I put on the new The Glorious Sundays album, *New Episode Every Sunday*, and therein started the routine that would define my journeys to and from group therapy every Thursday.

This album, *NEES*, is most famous for The Incident, obviously. It's not exactly an unknown moment in the band's history, even people who had never heard of TGS had heard of The Incident, the moment when James Chase lost his way.

Momentarily. Momentarily lost his way.

He hadn't been happy with the album as he felt it was poppier than anything TGS had done before, and he, it was rumoured, wanted TGS to retain the ambient, post-rock, disparate sounds the band was known for. The label, however, wanted a pop-rock album, something to push them into the charts and out of the underground. Apparently James wanted to fight this, wanted to protest their desire, wanted to refuse, but the band weren't keen on the idea. They'd gone too far to throw it away over label beef.

Tuocs Onej was now a permanent member of the band and had a voice in the way it was run, and they were caught between siding with the label or the lead singer. Amme was lost between the 'love of [her] life' and a career, and settling on pushing for the career. Tommy Six couldn't care less; he wanted the fame and fortune, and was willing to lose a friendship for it.

Barely three days after recording on *New Episode Every Sunday* ended, the polished pop sounds now confirmed on the master, James Chase had his infamous moment. James Chase was seen butt naked sat in the middle of a road outside of Exeter, weeping uncontrollably.

New Episode Every Sunday come out at the end of 2015, on New Year's Eve and I didn't get a chance to listen to it until my 27th birthday a month later, when somebody generously bought me the record - marble splatter with a free download code so I could jam out to it on car journeys.

NEES isn't the present I remember most from that birthday, in fact I don't even remember when or how I opened it. The only present that stood out that year was from one of my brothers: a cushion.[1]

---

1   To understand the dynamics of this present, I first have to explain a need I've had, since I was about seven years old, to own a certain cushion. It was a gold cushion I'd seen in the local, independently-run fabric shop in Redruth. I don't know why I adored it and desired it so, but I was young and I just felt like I needed it. So I saved my pocket money, week after week, until I could afford it. When other kids bought sweets I bought none, when they bought toys I went without. We couldn't afford much anyway, stone broke that we were, but that £1 a week I saved relentlessly until I could afford the gold cushion. And when I walked into the store, on the day I had enough, the cushion was gone, never to be seen again. I don't think my brother knew this story, and I don't think they had any negative intentions, but that memory played a part in this distinctly unusual response from myself.

Upon seeing the cushion I had a panic attack, like I'd never had before. The cushion was relatively small, an oblong oval shape, with an image printed on it. The image of my face.

I looked at myself on this cushion and could not handle what I was seeing, I saw myself in a new way and a way that I didn't like. I wanted to destroy it, I wanted to smash it to pieces and burn the remnants. I hated everything about it, the proportions, the shape, that face looking back at me. It was hideous and I broke.

Emma held me for hours as I sobbed beyond the point of being able to bring any oxygen into my system; I veered between panic attack and asthma attack. It was, and still remains, one of the worst sights I'd ever seen: my own face from a perspective not my own.

This was the point where I knew I needed help. This is the point where I realised how unhealthy it was to hate myself so much I wanted to hurt or kill myself.

Since there is so litle to say about *NEES*, most of the history, oral and written, focuses on the band's relationship during this period. But very little goes into any depth about the mental health issues James Chase was experiencing at the time. He had become a media poster boy for pop-rock, and his engagement to Amme was used by the media to sell copies of every two-bit rag going.

Like Kanye West and Britney Spears, the journalists weren't interested or invested in examining the culture of celebrity that led to the breakdown. Instead, the mental torture of the individual worked to ensure sales, and that was enough to globalise their illness and weaponise mental health as an economically profitable illness.

James Chase recently lost his father, a man he never knew nor cared for, but it manifested in a double grief, for the man he lost, and for the potential of the man he lost. This, combined with the pressures of recording, culminated in an extensive battle with himself, one he was destined to lose. Had the journalists done a bit more than surround him for photos, they might have seen the fragile shell of a man who had everything except what he actually wanted.

> I'm burning at both ends
> I'm counting down my friends
> I've lost the life I thought I had
> this is where the estuary bends
>
> — 'Lead me down the Estuary' by The Glorious Sundays

I didn't talk for the first month of my group therapy. I sat and listened, nodded at the right times. I tried to absorb the stories and healing present in the room, but I wasn't ready to share.[2]

Eventually I spoke, I shared, I recovered. I am grateful to every voice in that room, every Thursday evening for two hours. I am grateful for the biscuits we shared and the coffees we drank, for every moment of connection and health we promoted. It was there that I became capable of being Aaron, and it was there that I truly found the strength to forgive myself first, and others second.[3]

---

2   For what I hope is obvious reasons, I won't be mentioning the names or stories of anybody else who was present in group therapy.

3   I think it comes across as cliche to 'forgive yourself' but when I finally found that, that ability to forgive myself, I finally began to heal. I had to accept that I wasn't to blame for all the years of abuse and violence, and I wasn't weak for allowing it to happen. I was brave for still being here, and I could forgive myself for the pain I put myself through.

- Aaron Kent -

In Memory of...

_____

2016

In memory of...

B-sides and Demos.
Or, a return to normality was
only possible with a break from
putting our lives on the line.

Released only one year after *New Episode Every Sunday*, *In Memory of...* was a collection of b-sides and demos from almost 10 years of The Glorious Sundays.

Initially fans believed the rumours of James Chase's demse were true, that he had passed away and was the individual who the album was in memory of. Yet it soon became clear that James Chase was not only alive and well, but in fact better than he had ever been and the band were presenting this album as a eulogy to themselves.[1]

A lot of fans felt it had been on the cards for a while, considering they released two albums a year since 2007, James Chase's well-documented issues, and Tommy Six's desire to leave the limelight. This didn't make it any less disappointing when James Chase broke a three-month silence to record a video of himself, uploaded to Twitter, announcing the end of the band.

---

1   This clearly wouldn't last, as October 2020 saw them return with a new record, but the signs all pointed towards this collection of throwaways being the complete, final TGS.

Songs to Sing on your Deathbed

2020

On 7th October 2020, I was at work. It was a fairly typical day in a COVID world: socially distanced English teaching. This was actually more difficult than Zoom teaching, but we all made it work. At lunch I popped out to send some post, and that's pretty much the last thing I remember.

My brain bled. I later learnt I passed out in a colleague's office, and the on-site medic looked after me while an air ambulance was called out.[1] I was taken to the local hospital, where the set-up wasn't sufficient, before I was taken to Heath Hospital in Cardiff.

I don't remember the next week or so; it's a complete blank in my memory. Emma had to prepare herself to raise two children alone, and considered what songs I would want played at my funeral. If I was fortunate enough to live it wouldn't necessarily be as the person I had been before.

---

1   The medic is a former paramedic, who I owe my life to.

During this period of my life, The Glorious Sundays released a new, completely unexpected, six-track record.

I didn't listen to it in the hospital.

I didn't listen to it when I returned home in November.

I didn't listen to it in December.

I had enough about me to be able to bear music. Loud sounds made me uncomfortable for some time, and the headaches hung around for an extended period after my hospitalisation. But *finally*, in January, shortly before my 32nd birthday as soon as I was capable, I sat in my office and put *Songs to Sing on your Deathbed* on the speakers.

It's a bizarre experience to wake up in a hospital with no recollection of how or why you are in there. The bed next to me had an older guy who chatted to me like we'd been friends for years.[2] I later learnt I had been fairly chatty in the few days before I became cognitively aware.[3]

I missed my children and my wife dearly. Emma sent me a video of Rue telling me she loved me and I watched it a few dozens times a day, and made it the last thing I watched every night before I went to sleep. She also sent a video of Otis clapping which was in regular rotation alongside Rue's video. I was lost without my family, and it was a strange sort of juxtaposition to have been so desperate to die years earlier, only to be so desperate to cling to life now.

---

2   He loved submarines and the NFL, so I found him remarkably easy to talk to.
3   After my release in January, I went in for an angiogram - this is an operation where they made a cut in my groin, and then inserted a catheter wire into my femoral artery and guided it up through my arteries, past my neck, and into my brain, where they released a dye into my head. The doctors and nurses and technicians frequently proclaimed it was good to see me looking so healthy. I spoke with them, but for the most part, I had no idea who they were. Just staff I had seemingly conversed with during my blank days.

I have a sort of theory about death.[4] When we die, our consciousness transfers to another dimension or universe or timeline, where we are healthy. So we carry on living after we die and leave behind our previous shells for those in the other timeline to mourn. I know this isn't likely, and I don't actually believe it in a real sense, but it is something I often think about.

I often think about the grief left behind in the many timelines where I didn't make it. The timeline where my appendicitus killed me at 16, where I jumped off the balcony at 12, where my twisted bowel killed me at 30, where the brain haemorrhage killed me at 32, where I succesfully drove my car into a wall at 24, where the submarine sunk at 20. This puts me three deaths short of a permanent death, averaging one every five years.

---

4   I've named it the 'Mario Theory'.

Songs to Sing on your Deathbed is a six track album, with each song being a tribute to a studio album by the band. It's a 35-minute album taking the form of a reprise of their entire back catalogue. It's a whole meldoic release with its own musicality, but it glitches in and out of their previous hits, picking up and realtering past lyrics, a final bow at the curtain.

'Traversing all I've lost
took two shots before I dropped
Call me home when I sing of my second-best
I'm better now, better now at my best'

'I'm shoulder deep in your swimming pool
I held on so I didn't drown
I heard the bells ding dong the witch is dead
I saw the iron fist fall down.'

'I'm breaking ground in broken sleep
broken by these car crash dreams
this is the year I stand my ground
Amme can you hear me, I've been calling clearly
Winter gave me composure
I'm counting all my bullets as closure'

'Keep it together
the loaded sky is getting better
those words have finally come true'

'You are the path adventure brings
you are the reason the blackbird sings
I'll keep you close, near the end
my broken wings you can mend'

'I burnt myself at both ends
I counted down all my friends
I've learnt to love the time we spend
this is where the discography ends'

- Aaron Kent -

Acknowledgements

This was a tough thing to write, as I've never really written about these aspects of my life so openly, but it's a bit of a weight off my shoulders.Thank you to Cathleen Allyn Conway for her excellent editorial eye.

Thank you to Emma for saving me. Thank you to Rue for saving me. Thank you to Otis for saving me. Thank you to CRASAC for saving me. Thank you to The Glorious Sundays for saving me.

- Aaron Kent -

LAY OUT YOUR GLORIOUS SUNDAYS

CPSIA information can be obtained
at www.ICGtesting.com
Printed in the USA
LVHW072310070222
710476LV00011B/556

9 781913 642228